STORIES TO TEACH CHI DIGITAL CITIZENSHIP INTERNET MATURITY SKILLS.

ALL PARENTS ARE WORRIED ABOUT THEIR CHILDREN'S INTERNET MISUSE AND OVER USE. IN THIS BOOK I HAVE WRITTEN STORIES AROUND THE THREATS AND RISKS AS WELL AS THE OPPORTUNITIES AVAILABLE ON THE INTERNET.

DR. GEETANJALI JHA

Made with ♥ on the Notion Press Platform
www.notionpress.com

Dear Readers, parents, and children,

Hi, I am Dr. Geetanjali Jha, I am presenting a new kind of storybook for you to read together.

Since times immemorial parents have read or narrated stories to their children at bedtime.

These stories help the parents and children to spend time together and develop a deep bond of tenderness, love, and trust. These bedtime stories had some lessons which laid the foundation of an ethical and virtuous code of conduct in the minds of the children. Like "honesty is the best policy", "a stitch in time saves nine" etc. These subconsciously learned lessons have helped generations of kids to grow up into wholesome individuals.

In the 21st century, all those life skills and morals still hold good, but their reach has to be extended to the digital world as well.

A grown-up individual might be capable of learning the right and wrong of the digital world through training and experience, but while growing up our children need hand-holding in this regard.

Stories serve as a non-threatening and vicarious means of learning acceptable and unacceptable behaviour and its consequences.

So, as a counselling psychologist working as a Digital Citizenship and Internet Maturity Educator, as well as a Digital Parenting Expert, I have written some short stories for inculcating Netiquette and digital discipline in the minds of young children.

I believe that by the time children come to the appropriate age for unsupervised Internet and social media usage, it is already too late to teach them the pros and cons of the cyber world. Thus, this book caters to children in middle and late childhood. An age when their minds are curious, responsive, and highly impressionable. At this age, they are able to understand the consequences of good and bad behaviour and want to be appreciated by their parents. So it is a golden period for parents and children for developing a strong bond for communicating about matters related to the Internet, and for preparing them for what comes in the future.

Please feel free to explain and elaborate upon the stories given in this book. Let your kid ask you questions about them, and be prepared to answer those in a manner that your kid understands.

I hope my book serves the purpose for which it is written and inculcates Internet Maturity in the coming generation of young adults.

Happy Reading!

Love,

Dr. Geetanjali Jha

P.S. The characters and situations in these stories are fictitious, but the lessons are real.

Contents

CHAPTER ONE

"How Sarah stood up against Cyberbullying"

Once upon a time, in a magical kingdom far away, there lived a kind and curious princess named Sarah. She loved to explore the kingdom and make new friends, but one day, something terrible happened.

Sarah met a new friend named Jack, who seemed very nice at first. They would talk and play games together, but soon Sarah noticed that Jack would say mean things to her and make fun of her online. She felt hurt and alone and didn't know what to do.

Image by Freepik

Sarah's best friend, Prince Edward, noticed that she was upset and asked her what was wrong. Sarah told him about Jack's behavior and Prince Edward was shocked. He knew that this was something called cyberbullying and that it was not okay.

Prince Edward helped Sarah block Jack and report his behavior to the castle's cyber guardian, who helped to stop the bullying. Sarah felt much better but still felt a little sad.

Prince Edward knew that Sarah needed to talk to someone about her feelings, so he took her to see the castle's wise old wizard. The wizard listened to Sarah's story and helped her understand that it was not her fault and that she did nothing wrong. He also taught her how to be more assertive and stand up for herself, in case something like this ever happens again.

Sarah felt much better after talking to the wizard and Prince Edward. She learned that cyberbullying is not okay and that it's important to tell someone if it happens to you. She also learned that it's important to be kind to others because you never know what they may be going through.

With Prince Edward by her side, Sarah continued to explore the kingdom and make new friends, but she was more careful and aware of the cyberbullying threat. She became a role model to other children and helped many to stand up to cyberbullies and spread kindness online.

Write your thoughts, your child's questions, and insights in the space below.

CHAPTER TWO

"The Online Gaming Adventure"

Once upon a time, in a peaceful town, there lived a young boy named Surya. He was a curious and adventurous boy, who loved to explore and play games. One day, Surya discovered a new online game that caught his attention. It was called "Dragon Quest" and it was a very fun and exciting game. Surya played it every day, for hours on end.

As the days passed, Surya's love for the game grew stronger. He stopped going out with his friends, stopped playing sports, and stopped doing his homework. He would spend all his time playing the game and would get very angry when someone tried to take him away from it.

His parents noticed that something was wrong with Surya. They tried to talk to him about it, but he would always say that he was fine and that he just really loved the game. They were worried about him and decided to seek help from the village's wise old wizard.

The wizard listened to Surya's parents' concerns and knew that the boy was suffering from online gaming addiction. He knew that it was a serious problem and that something needed to be done about it. He suggested that Surya should take a break from the game for a while and try other activities that he used to enjoy.

He was reluctant at first, but he knew that the wizard was right. He decided to take a break from the game and try other activities. He started to go out with his friends again, play sports, and do his homework. He also started to spend more time with his family.

As the days passed, Surya realized that there were so many other things in life that were just as fun and exciting as the game. He also realized that he missed spending time with his friends and family. He was no longer addicted to the game and was happy and content with the things he was doing.

Surya's parents were very happy to see him happy again. They knew that it was all thanks to the wizard, who had helped their son to overcome his addiction.

From that day on, Surya enjoyed all the activities he used to do and still played games occasionally but in a balanced way, he learned the importance of balance and moderation in life. He became a role model to other children in the village, who learned from his experience to avoid falling prey to online gaming addiction.

Write your thoughts, your child's questions, and insights in the space below.

CHAPTER THREE

"Selfie Selfie Everywhere.."

Once upon a time, in a bustling city, there lived a young girl named Emily. Emily loved taking pictures of herself and posting them on social media. She loved the attention and the likes she would get from her friends and followers. She loved how it made her feel popular and important. Even when everyone was enjoying a day in the garden and participating in the work, Emily would be busy clicking selfies.

Images by upklyak on Freepik

As the days passed, Emily's addiction to taking selfies grew stronger. She would spend hours in front of the mirror, trying to find the perfect angle and the perfect lighting. She would take dozens of pictures of herself, just to find the perfect one to post online.

Her friends and family noticed that something was wrong with Emily. They tried to talk to her about it, but she would always say that she just loved taking pictures and that there was nothing wrong with it. They were worried about her and decided to seek help from the city's wise old wizard.

The wizard listened to Emily's friends' and family's concerns and knew that the girl was suffering from selfie addiction. He knew that it was a serious problem and that something needed to be done about it. He suggested that Emily should take a break from taking selfies for a while and try other activities that she used to enjoy.

Emily was reluctant at first, but she knew that the wizard was right. She decided to take a break from taking selfies and try other activities. She started to spend more time with her friends and family, read books, and volunteer in her community.

As the days passed, Emily realized that there were so many other things in life that were just as fun and fulfilling as taking selfies. She also realized that she missed spending time with her friends and family and doing things that made her feel good inside. She was no longer addicted to taking selfies and was happy and content with the things she was doing.

Emily's friends and family were very happy to see her happy again. They knew that it was all thanks to the wizard, who had helped her to overcome her addiction.

From that day on, Emily still took pictures of herself but in a balanced way, she learned the importance of balance and moderation in life. She became a role model to other children in the city, who learned from her experience to avoid falling prey to selfie addiction.

Write your thoughts, your child's questions, and insights in the space below.

CHAPTER FOUR

"The Screen Adventure"

Once upon a time, in a small town, there lived a young boy named Max. Max loved to play video games, watch videos, and browse the Internet. He would spend hours in front of his screens every day, and he loved it.

As the days passed, Max's excessive screen usage started to take a toll on his physical health. He began to experience eye strain, headaches, and back pain from sitting in front of screens for long periods of time. He started to feel tired and weak all the time, and he couldn't understand why.

Image by ucoyxmasayun on Freepik

His parents noticed that something was wrong with Max. They tried to talk to him about it, but he would always say that he was fine and that he just loved playing games and watching videos. They were worried about him and decided to seek help from the town's wise old doctor.

The doctor examined Max and discovered that he was suffering from poor posture, eye strain, and lack of physical activity due to excessive screen usage. He knew that it was a serious problem and that something needed to be done about it. He suggested that Max should take regular breaks from screens, practice good posture and engage in physical activities.

Max was reluctant at first, but he knew that the doctor was right. He decided to take regular breaks from screens and engage in physical activities. He started to play sports, go for walks and engage in other activities that required him to move his body.

As the days passed, Max realized that there were so many other things in life that were just as fun and exciting as playing video games and watching videos. He also realized that his body felt better and stronger. He was no longer addicted to screens and was happy and content with the things he was doing.

Max's parents were very happy to see him happy and healthy again. They knew that it was all thanks to the doctor, who had helped their son to overcome his excessive screen usage.

From that day on, Max still enjoyed playing video games and watching videos but in a balanced way, he learned the importance of balance and moderation in life. He became a role model to other children in the town, who learned from his experience to avoid ruining their physical health due to excessive screen usage.

Write your thoughts, your child's questions, and insights in the space below.

CHAPTER FIVE

"Timmy and Social Media"

Once upon a time, there was a young child named Timmy. Timmy was a bright student with a passion for learning new things. However, he struggled to focus on his academics because of his addiction to social media.

Timmy spent hours each day scrolling through his social media feeds, constantly checking for new updates and notifications. He became so engrossed in the endless stream of posts and images that he found it difficult to concentrate on his schoolwork.

His grades began to suffer, and his teachers and parents became increasingly worried. They tried to intervene, setting limits on his social media usage and monitoring his online activity. But Timmy found ways to circumvent their attempts to control his addiction.

One day, Timmy's teacher assigned a difficult project that required a lot of research and concentration. Timmy knew that he needed to focus if he wanted to succeed, but he found it hard to pull himself away from his phone.

Image by Freepik

As he sat at his desk, staring at the project instructions, he realized that his social media addiction was holding him back. He made the decision to delete all of his social media accounts and focus on his schoolwork.

With his mind clear and free from distractions, Timmy was able to complete his project with ease. His grades improved, and he felt a sense of pride and accomplishment.

Timmy learned a valuable lesson that day. He realized that while social media can be a fun and entertaining way to connect with others, it's important to be able to control one's usage and not let it take over one's life.

Write your thoughts, your child's questions, and insights in the space below.

CHAPTER SIX

"The Hidden Dangers of Internet Overuse"

Once upon a time, there was a young child named Sophie. She was an intelligent and curious child who loved exploring the world around her. However, as she grew older, she began to spend more and more time on the Internet.

Sophie spent hours each day on her phone and computer, scrolling through social media, watching videos, and chatting with friends. Her parents and teachers were initially happy that she was staying connected and staying informed. But as time passed, they began to notice changes in Sophie's behavior.

She became more withdrawn, anxious, and depressed. She was losing interest in the things she used to enjoy and was struggling to focus on her studies. Her grades began to suffer, and her teachers and parents became increasingly worried.

They tried to intervene and set limits on her Internet usage, but Sophie found ways to circumvent their attempts to control her usage. Her mental health continued to deteriorate, and she was unable to find peace and happiness.

It was only when Sophie's parents sought help from a counsellor that they realized the extent of the problem. The counsellor helped Sophie to understand the negative effects of Internet overuse on her mental health and how to regain control of her online habits. The counsellor taught her self-discipline techniques, made her realize the importance of exercising and mindfulness.

With the help of her counsellor, Sophie was able to reduce her Internet usage and regain her interest in the things she used to enjoy. She was able to improve her grades and her mental health.

Sophie learned a valuable lesson that day. She realized that while the Internet can be a powerful tool for connecting and learning, it's important to be able to control one's usage and not let it take over one's life.

Write your thoughts, your child's questions, and insights in the space below.

CHAPTER SEVEN

"A Child's Accidental Encounter with Cybercrime"

Once upon a time, there was a young child named Jack. Jack was a curious and adventurous child who loved to explore the online world. One day, while browsing the Internet, he stumbled upon a website that promised free games and prizes.

Excited by the prospect of winning something, he clicked on the website and began to play the games. However, as he played, he started to notice some strange things happening on his computer.

He was prompted to enter personal information and download suspicious software.

Image by pikisuperstar on Freepik

Unknowingly, Jack had accidentally become a part of cybercrime. The website was actually a scam that was designed to steal personal information and spread malware. Jack's computer was infected with a virus, and his personal information was stolen.

As the days passed, Jack began to notice strange charges on his parent's credit card, and he received calls and emails from strangers. His parents were shocked and worried when they found out what had happened.

They immediately contacted the authorities and took steps to protect their personal information and fix the damage caused by the virus. They also educated Jack about Internet safety and the importance of being cautious when browsing the web.

Jack learned a valuable lesson that day. He realized that the Internet can be a dangerous place and that it's important to be aware of the risks and protect oneself from cybercrime.

Write your thoughts, your child's questions, and insights in the space below.

CHAPTER EIGHT

"A Teenager's Journey to Building a Positive Online Reputation"

Once upon a time, there was a teenager named Sarah. Sarah was an ambitious and hardworking student who had always dreamed of attending a prestigious university. She worked tirelessly throughout high school to maintain a high academic grades and participate in extracurricular activities.

However, Sarah had not given much thought to her online presence. She had an active social media account and often posted pictures and comments without thinking of the consequences. She had no idea that her online actions could impact her future.

As the time to apply to college approached, Sarah's guidance counsellor told her that she had a strong chance of getting into her dream school. However, when the admissions committee looked at her online presence, they saw pictures of her at parties and questionable comments on her social media pages. They also saw that her online presence was not matching her application.

They denied her admission, citing that her online reputation did not reflect the values of the university. Sarah was devastated. She had lost the opportunity to attend her dream school because of her carelessness online.

Feeling regretful, Sarah decided to take control of her online presence. She cleaned up her social media profiles, set them to private, and began to be more mindful of her online actions.

Sarah learned a valuable lesson that day. She realized that the Internet is a permanent place and whatever we post or share there stays there forever and it can have a big impact on our future opportunities.

She took guidance from her school seniors and her academic counsellor, who helped her build a good, strong online reputation that showcased her skills and achievements and was in sync with her application. With consistent effort in managing her online reputation, she applied for admission to colleges once again. And even though it took some time, she was able to get admission to a very good college of her choice.

Image by pikisuperstar on Freepik

Write your thoughts, your child's questions, and insights in the space below.

CHAPTER NINE

"The Consequences of Plagiarism: A Student's Struggle with Academic Dishonesty"

Once upon a time, there was a boy named Alex. Alex was a hardworking student who had always been interested in science and technology. When his class was assigned a project on the latest advancements in Artificial Intelligence, Alex was excited to dive in and do some research.

However, instead of spending hours researching and writing, Alex decided to take a shortcut. He found an article online that covered the same topic as his project and copied large portions of it into his own work. He thought that no one would notice, and he would get a good grade.

But, when he submitted his project, his teacher immediately recognized the plagiarism. She gave him a failing grade as he had copied his work from another source

Image by Freepik

She confronted Alex and explained to him that plagiarism is a serious offense and is considered academic dishonesty. She rejected his project and gave him a failing grade for the assignment.

Feeling ashamed and guilty, Alex apologized to his teacher and admitted that he had made a mistake. He was given the opportunity to redo the project but with a stricter deadline and guidelines this time. He had to start from scratch and put in a lot of effort to make sure his project was original and his own work.

Alex learned a valuable lesson that day. He realized that plagiarism is not only dishonest, but it also undermines the integrity of one's work and can have serious consequences. He also learned that hard work and dedication are always worth it in the end.

Write your thoughts, your child's questions, and insights in the space below.

CHAPTER TEN

"What happened when Tommy shared too much on social media"

Once upon a time, there was a child named Tommy. Tommy was a playful and outgoing child who loved sharing his life on social media. He had an active account on various platforms and would regularly post pictures and updates about his family, friends, and school. He thought it was fun and harmless.

However, his parents began to notice that Tommy was sharing too much information online. He was posting pictures of their home address, pictures of his family, and pictures of his school. Pictures of what he was eating, buying, and his activities, he shared everything on social media He was also sharing his school schedule and the places he went with his family.

Image by brgfx on Freepik

One day, Tommy's parents received a phone call from the school principal. They were informed that Tommy's posts had attracted the attention of a stranger who had been attempting to contact him. The stranger had even gone to the school and asked for him by name.

Tommy's parents were shocked and worried. They immediately took steps to protect their family's privacy and safety. They changed the privacy settings on Tommy's accounts, and they had a talk with him about Internet safety and the importance of being cautious about the information shared online.

Tommy learned a valuable lesson that day. He realized that the Internet is not a private place and that whatever we post online can be seen by anyone. He also learned that it is important to be mindful of the information shared online and to be aware of the potential risks of oversharing.

Write your thoughts, your child's questions, and insights in the space below.

CHAPTER ELEVEN

"The Art of Resilience: How a Child's Creative Spirit Triumphed over Online Trolling"

Once upon a time, there was a child named Mia. Mia was a creative and artistic child who loved to express herself through art and writing. She often posted her work on social media, hoping to get feedback and inspiration from others.

However, soon after she started posting her work online, she began to receive negative and hurtful comments from strangers. They criticized her work, calling it bad and talentless. They trolled her, making fun of her and encouraging her to give up.

Mia was hurt and confused by the negative comments. She began to question her own talent and creativity. She felt like she didn't have the courage to continue sharing her work online.

She confided in her family, who helped her to understand that not everyone will have the same taste and appreciation for her work and that trolling and negativity is a common problem on the Internet. They encouraged her to not let the trolls get to her and to keep creating.

With her family's support and encouragement, Mia decided to not let the trolls win. She continued to share her work online, and she also found a community of like-minded individuals who appreciated and supported her art.

Mia learned a valuable lesson that day. She realized that the Internet can be a harsh place, but it's important to not let the negativity of others bring her down. She also learned that it's important to surround herself with people who support and encourage her creativity.

Write your thoughts, your child's questions, and insights in the space below.

CHAPTER TWELVE

"Falling Prey to Online Manipulation: A Child's Journey of Recognizing and Overcoming Brainwashing"

Once upon a time, there was a child named David. David was a curious and open-minded child who loved exploring the world around him. He spent a lot of time online, learning new things and connecting with people from all over the world. However, he didn't always use his critical thinking when interacting with others online.

One day, David came across a person online who presented themselves as a friendly and knowledgeable individual. They struck up a conversation and over time, this person began to share ideas and beliefs that David had never heard before. They were persuasive and charismatic, and David found himself becoming increasingly drawn to their ideas.

Without realizing it, David was falling prey to a stranger who was brainwashing him. They were manipulating him into believing things that were not true and encouraging him to act in ways that were harmful to himself and others. David's parents noticed a change in his behavior and became worried.

When they confronted him about it, David was shocked and saddened to realize that he had been manipulated by a stranger. With the help of his parents and a counsellor, David learned how to critically evaluate information and sources online and how to recognize manipulative behavior. He also learned how to set healthy boundaries and to speak up when something didn't feel right.

David learned a valuable lesson that day. He realized that the Internet is a powerful tool, but it's important to be critical and cautious when interacting with others online. He also learned that it's important to have a strong sense of self and to trust his instincts when something doesn't feel right.

Write your thoughts, your child's questions, and insights in the space below.

CHAPTER THIRTEEN

"How Jane fought against Cyberstalking"

Once upon a time, there was a teenager named Jane. Jane was a friendly and outgoing teenager who loved to connect with people online. She had a social media account and she would often share her thoughts, feelings, and pictures with her friends and followers.

However, one day she started receiving strange messages from someone she didn't know. The messages were friendly at first, but they soon became more persistent, and the person began to ask for personal information and pictures. Jane felt uncomfortable with the attention, but she didn't know how to respond.

Image by pikisuperstar on Freepik

The messages continued, and the person started to appear on her social media accounts, her school, and even her house. They would leave messages and gifts, and they would try to contact her friends and family. Jane started to feel scared and trapped, she didn't know what to do or who to trust.

Jane's parents noticed her distress and helped her to understand that she was being stalked online. They helped her to report the stalking incident to the authorities, and they also set up privacy settings on her social media accounts. They also sought help from a counsellor who helped them to cope with the trauma of being stalked.

Jane learned a valuable lesson that day. She realized that the Internet can be a powerful tool, but it's important to be mindful of the information shared online and to be aware of the potential risks of cyberstalking. She also learned that it's important to trust her instincts, speak up and get help when something doesn't feel right.

Write your thoughts, your child's questions, and insights in the space below.

CHAPTER FOURTEEN

"The Importance of Digital Citizenship: A Child's Journey to Creating and Sharing Content Responsibly"

Once upon a time, there was a child named Alex. Alex was a curious and tech-savvy child who was well-educated in Digital Citizenship. He understood the importance of creating and sharing digital content responsibly and ethically.

He knew that it was important to protect his own privacy and the privacy of others when posting online. He also knew how to verify the information he found online and not believe everything he read.

Alex was also well-versed in the laws and guidelines governing digital content, and he always made sure to give credit where credit was due. He never plagiarized or shared copyrighted material without permission.

Not only that, but Alex was also a creator himself. He loved to create videos, music, and design and he always made sure to ask for permission when using someone else's content. He also shared his own work online, but always did so with the understanding that it could be seen by anyone and that it was important to be mindful of the impact it could have.

Alex's digital literacy and awareness earned him respect and admiration from his peers, teachers, and the online community. His digital footprint was a shining example of how to be a responsible digital citizen.

Write your thoughts, your child's questions, and insights in the space below.

CHAPTER FIFTEEN

"The Power of Open Courseware and MOOCs: A Teenager's Journey to Earning Certificates and Building a Stronger Future."

Once upon a time, there was a teenager named Sita. Sita was an ambitious and hardworking student who always had a passion for learning. She was always looking for ways to expand her knowledge and skills. That's when she came across the concept of Open Courseware (OCWs) and Massive Open Online Courses (MOOCs).

She discovered that these resources offered a wide range of classes and courses from top universities and institutions around the world, available for free or at a low cost. Sita took advantage of these opportunities and began to explore a variety of subjects that interested her.

She learned about programming, design, business, and many other subjects. She was able to earn certificates and badges for her achievements, which she added to her resume and online portfolio. She also gained valuable knowledge and skills that helped her in her studies and future career.

Sita's hard work and dedication paid off as her certificates and badges helped her to stand out from her peers when applying to colleges and internships. Her OCWs and MOOC certificates also helped her to land a job after graduation.

Image by Freepik

Sita's experience was an example that online education can be a valuable resource for anyone looking to expand their knowledge and skills, regardless of their background or location.

Write your thoughts, your child's questions, and insights in the space below.

CHAPTER SIXTEEN

"The Importance of Digital Citizenship and Internet Maturity and How a Teenager Avoided Online Threats and Risks"

Once upon a time, there was a teenager named Emily. Emily was a smart and responsible teenager who had been educated in Digital Citizenship and Internet Maturity from a young age. She knew the importance of being safe and responsible when using the Internet.

She understood the potential risks and threats that come with being online, such as cyberbullying, online predators, and the spread of misinformation. Emily also knew the importance of protecting her personal information and privacy online.

She was careful about the information she shared online, never posting personal details or pictures that could put her at risk. She also knew how to spot and report suspicious or inappropriate behavior online. She also made sure to verify the information she found online, using multiple sources to ensure its accuracy.

Emily also knew the importance of being a responsible digital citizen, treating others online with respect and kindness, and not engaging in cyberbullying or spreading misinformation.

Thanks to her education in Digital Citizenship and Internet Maturity, Emily was able to navigate the Internet safely and responsibly. She was able to enjoy all the benefits of the Internet without falling prey to its potential risks.

Image by brgfx on Freepik

Write your thoughts, your child's questions, and insights in the space below.

CHAPTER SEVENTEEN

"The Importance of Online Reputation: How a Child's Responsible Use of the Internet Led to Scholarship and Internship Opportunities"

Once upon a time, there was a child named Mia. Mia was an ambitious and hardworking child who always had a passion for learning. She was also very conscious about her online reputation and the impact it could have on her future.

From a young age, Mia understood the importance of being responsible and respectful online. She was careful about the information she shared, and she always made sure to treat others with kindness and respect. She also knew how to recognize and avoid online scams, fake news, and misinformation.

As she grew older, Mia's online reputation began to pay off. She applied for a scholarship and got accepted because of her good online reputation, her scholarship provider saw her as a responsible, trustworthy, and respectful individual. She was also offered an internship with a well-known company due to her good online reputation, which helped her to gain valuable work experience and connections in her desired field.

Image by photoroyalty on Freepik

Mia's experience showed the importance of maintaining a good online reputation and how it can benefit one's personal and professional life. It also showed that with the right approach, one can use the Internet to make a positive impact and open doors for opportunities.

Write your thoughts, your child's questions, and insights in the space below.

Your feedback is valuable to me, so please scan the QR code below to fill up a short form for the same.

Thank you for your time and support.
Regards,
Dr. Geetanjali Jha

Ingram Content Group UK Ltd.
Milton Keynes UK
UKHW050406230323
419018UK00003B/73